The Thirty-Six Stratagems for Young Minds

The Clever Peach Trick

Edited by **KaDa Gushi** and **Hongyan Mao**
Illustrated by **Chen Wei Studio**

Books Beyond Boundaries
ROYAL COLLINS

During the Spring and Autumn Period, the State of Qi was home to three mighty generals: Tian Kaijiang, Gu Yezi, and Gongsun Jie. They were known as the Three Heroes of Qi, unmatched in strength and courage.

Because of their great victories, Duke Jing of Qi granted them noble titles and honored them in court.

齊
齊
齊

Tian Kaijiang had a fiery red face, large eyes like bronze bells, and a sharp, hooked nose like an eagle's beak.

As the commander during Qi's invasion of the State of Xu, he never lost a battle, slaying Xu's top general and capturing over five hundred enemy soldiers. His victories intimidated Xu, Tan, and Ju, forcing them to form an alliance with Qi.

Gu Yezi had a face as dark as ink, a thick black beard, and hands as strong as iron hooks. His strength was legendary.

Once, while accompanying Duke Jing of Qi across the Yellow River, a giant turtle suddenly surfaced, biting the duke's chariot horse and dragging it into the water.

Without hesitation, Gu Yezi drew his sword and leaped into the river. Moments later, he resurfaced—holding the horse's tail in one hand and the turtle's severed head in the other.

Gongsun Jie had a dark purple complexion, sharp triangular eyes, and a build as strong as an ox. His strength was beyond measure.

One day, while hunting with Duke Jing, a ferocious tiger leaped from the forest, charging straight at the duke. The royal guards fled in terror, but Gongsun Jie stood his ground. He grabbed the tiger's neck with one hand and struck its head with the other, killing it with his bare fists.

The three generals were inseparable, bonded like brothers by their shared love of martial arts. However, their pride grew unchecked.

Since they had little formal education, they believed their military achievements made them superior to scholars and officials. They refused to bow to Prime Minister Yan Ying, and no court official dared to offend them. Worse still, they carried swords to court, making even Duke Jing himself uneasy.

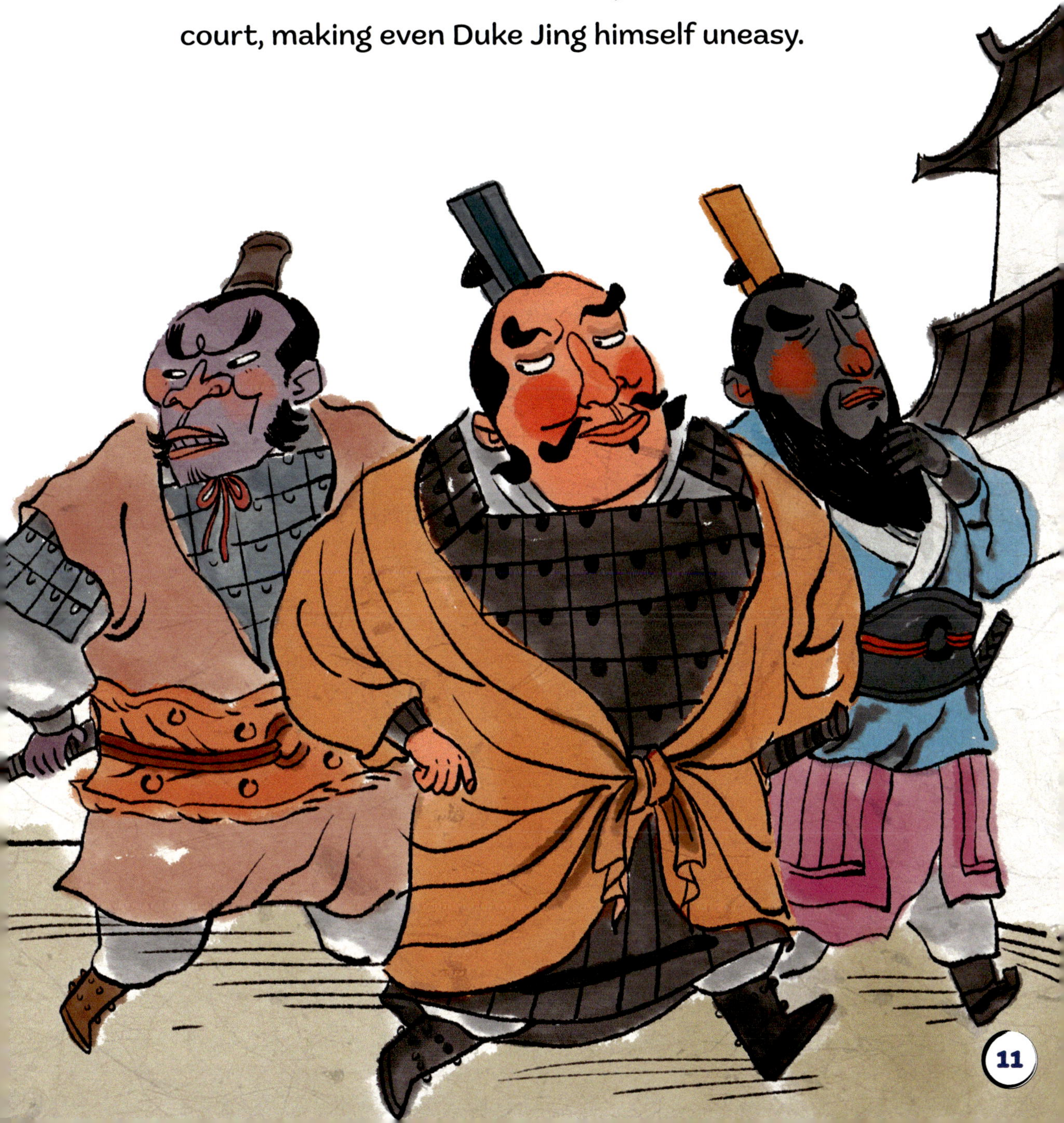

One day, Yan Ying approached Duke Jing and said, “Your Majesty, these three generals may be powerful, but they show no respect. They could one day become a threat to your throne.”

Duke Jing sighed. “I fear the same, but they are too strong. Who could possibly defeat them?”

Yan Ying smiled. “Your Majesty, they rely on their strength but lack wisdom. With a simple trick, I can make them destroy each other.”

Not long after, Duke Zhao of Lu visited the State of Qi, bringing his Prime Minister Shusun Chuo. Duke Jing held a grand banquet in their honor, with Yan Ying overseeing the event. The three generals stood below the royal steps, swords strapped to their sides.

As the feast went on, Yan Ying suddenly stood and said, “Your Majesty, the golden peaches in the royal garden have ripened. I shall bring some to celebrate this occasion.”

A moment later, Yan Ying returned, carrying a tray with six large peaches—each as big as a bowl and sweetly fragrant.

Duke Jing boasted, “This peach tree came from a distant land and has grown for over thirty years. It blossoms beautifully every year, but only bears a few peaches.”

Duke Jing of Qi, Duke Zhao of Lu, and the two Prime Ministers each took a peach, leaving only two peaches on the tray.

Yan Ying turned to the three generals and said, “Your Majesty, why not reward these last two peaches to the most deserving heroes of Qi?”

Duke Jing agreed. “You three, tell us—who has the greatest achievements? The two with the highest merit shall receive the peaches.”

The moment he finished speaking, Gongsun Jie stepped forward. “I once saved Your Majesty from a ferocious tiger while hunting. That is surely a great service!”

Yan Ying nodded. “Risking one’s life to save Your Majesty is a great achievement! You deserve a peach.”

Gongsun Jie proudly took a peach, drank a cup of wine, and stood aside, looking pleased with himself.

Next, Gu Yezi spoke. “Killing a tiger is no great feat! I once dived into the Yellow River to slay a giant turtle that had attacked Your Majesty’s chariot. Without me, you would have drowned!”

Duke Jing agreed. “Indeed, without your courage, I would not be here today. Your service is unmatched.”

Yan Ying handed the last peach to Gu Yezi, who took it with pride.

At that moment, Tian Kaijiang stepped forward, his expression dark. “I led the campaign against the State of Xu, defeating its army and capturing five hundred enemy soldiers. Because of me, Qi became more powerful, and the neighboring states of Tan and Ju submitted to our rule. Tell me, is my achievement not greater than theirs?”

Yan Ying calmly replied, “General Tian, your victories have expanded the State of Qi beyond measure, far surpassing what these two have done. But . . . the peaches are gone. Perhaps next year, when the tree bears fruit again, you shall have one.”

Tian Kaijiang's face turned red with rage. He grabbed his sword and roared, "Killing a tiger? Catching a turtle? Worthless! I risked my life on the battlefield, yet I am humiliated in front of two rulers! How can I live with this shame?"

Before anyone could react, he drew his sword and ended his own life.

Gongsun Jie gasped and looked at his peach. “I was given this for a small deed, while Tian Kaijiang, who led an entire war, was denied one? I was greedy, selfish, and blind to fairness! What honor is there in keeping this peach?”

With that, he, too, took his own life.

Seeing his two sworn brothers fall, Gu Yezi could not contain his sorrow. “We swore to live and die together! If they are gone, how can I stay behind?”

With a cry, he followed them in death.

In the end, Yan Ying never lifted a hand against the three generals. With only two peaches, Yan Ying turned their own pride into their downfall.

This strategy became known as “Kill with a Borrowed Knife”—a clever way to defeat enemies by making others strike in your place.

Historical Notes

Yan Ying

A famous diplomat and strategist of Qi. Despite his small stature, he was known for his sharp wit and quick thinking.

Duke Jing of Qi

The ruler of Qi during the Spring and Autumn period. Though he sought to govern well, he also enjoyed a life of luxury.

Shusun Chuo

He was a prime minister of Lu and was known for his diplomacy. He played a key role in alliances between states.

Moral of the Story True strength is not about fighting harder but thinking smarter. The greatest victories belong to those who use wisdom over force.

The State of Qi

Founded by Jiang Ziya, Qi became a major power in ancient China, known for its wealth and military strength.

Giant Turtle (大鼋)

A large turtle-like creature believed to live in deep waters. In ancient times, people feared them as river monsters.

Prime Minister (丞相)

A high-ranking official was in charge of governing the state and advising the king.

About the Editor

Mao Hongyan is the associate editor of *Happy Chinese Language and Composition*, a children's magazine. With a deep passion for children's literature, she is highly dedicated to children's growth and has extensive experience in children's book planning. She understands child psychology and cognitive development, crafting texts that align with young readers' psychological characteristics. Her works are beloved by children and parents alike. She has published *Interactive Sound Book: Fun with Chinese Idioms*, produced by Lelequ.

About the Illustrator

Chen Wei, born in 1979 in Taizhou, Jiangsu, graduated from the Design Department of Xi'an Academy of Fine Arts.

His notable picture books include *A New Resident in Kano Town*, *The Mice of Rose Villa*, and *The Frog and the Boy*. Among them, *The Frog and the Boy* won the Second Feng Zikai Children's Picture Book Award Jury Prize. His works have been translated and published in Taiwan, Hong Kong, and South Korea.

The Thirty-Six Stratagems for Young Minds: The Clever Peach Trick

Edited by KaDa Gushi and Hongyan Mao
Illustrated by Chen Wei Studio

First published in 2025 by Royal Collins Publishing Group Inc.
Groupe Publication Royal Collins Inc.
550-555 boul. René-Lévesque O Montréal (Québec) H2Z1B1 Canada

ISBN: 978-1-4878-1335-2

To find out more about our publications,
please visit www.royalcollins.com.